MY OWN BODY BREATHING

POEMS

ANNE CARMACK

©2020 Anne Carmack
All rights reserved.
Made in USA

First Edition

ISBN: 978-1-7350726-0-9

Cover design & layout by Heather Dakota

Wyrd & Wyld Publishing
Spokane, WA
www.heatherdakota.com

For Sarah and everything after—
because less is always more.

ANNE CARMACK

MY OWN BODY BREATHING

POEMS

First,
An old star became my body.

You are time now
Tall enough to touch the leaves on the trees
that have grown
while we weren't watching
while we all looked the other way

Woman,
I regard you with a reverence
that I used to save for saints

Man,
you speak in tongues of light
and liquid color

Wherever I've been touched
and loved
and hustled
I've been stained

You are not a ghost yet
but I see through you
flesh and memories
made to look like something else
twisted tight to make a life
with a mountain view for a mouth
and five fingers good for digging
and five more fingers for holding what you find

Outside the crowd is shouting
light blind and too lazy to run
they feel for the shade with their eyes closed
while you let your broken body burn

One day down the road
we will bury you
(they will carry you if I am not there)

And soft grass will grow over
the hole where they hide you
while your story untold
turns to seed

I've had glass in my foot for a week
and no one's noticed

Summer snuck up today
and hit us all on the head
so hard we're scared to sleep

Part of the sky was pink tonight
but the rest of it was blue
like the song
or the mood
or the day in other places
during seasons I don't even remember
In spaces that I always shared with you

I'm out here staring into nothingness,
she said,
because it's way too hot to go inside

I asked the moon to keep an eye on her
and he agreed

Somewhere along the path of totality
in the state where I grew up
they planned a parade
and ordered five hundred pairs of paper glasses
meant to protect you

Out in front of the school
a rented tent that was pitched before dawn
tricked the kids because it looked like a circus

I was seventeen hundred miles away
when it happened
by the time it arrived uninvited
like a hand
covering my eyes from behind
I was gone

Snake
Snake
Gone
You made me move too fast
Sucked me dry
I'm running now
Because you said to

Stop!

The light out here is blinding

Beloved
Beloved
I'm not hiding anymore
I have decided

Where have you gone?

In the dry heat of the distance
I see your black tail disappear
And slip back into the cracks
Made by the sun

Remember then
That it came to your house
And knocked on your door
And peeked in every window

Remember that it looked around
And called for you
And left a handwritten note by your bed
That you still have not opened
Even though it clearly says your name

The mulch is a mess
Full of cigarette butts
And pods from a plant I can't name
I assume someone still lives here
Ducking down behind drawn curtains
Yellow fingered
Yellow toothed

Stop
You know it's rude to stare
Or look too long at strangers on the street
I like to line up their strides with the songs that I am
writing
I like to imagine their mother's soft hands

When I was a little girl
I was afraid to hold my breath underwater
Because I didn't want to die
All the big kids called me chicken
And tried to push me in the pool

The joke's on them
I'm still alive

The last bad man I ever messed around with
Had the sugar lipped smile of a child
And a rusty ruined heart
His name was not a word
But the sound that a soul makes
When it is wrenched
From your ribs and shredded by sword
Not a screech or a scream
But a sigh so long
It starts to sound like your favorite love song

Floodtide or drought
It's the work of the wind
as it changes directions
when the rain comes again
(and it will, God willing)
the levels will rise
and if the dam isn't strong
we will drown

Outside the front door
the dark is wrestling with dawn
and will lose

All the girls like to say
that moon makes things happen
but I don't believe
that a rock can control me

I don't blame the sky anymore
I am free

Think about some things that rise:
Heat and helium
Bread baked by the mother
Of the man that raised you
Or the babysitter
Whose shin
You kicked hard
Before you hid in the closet
Until your mother came home and got angry

Do revolutionaries rise?

Do poets?

What is left for us to do down here
On our knees in the mud
Someone needs to say something
Someone needs to stop this, to shout

We are begging while we think about
Some other things that rise:
Tempers
Creeks
Sea levels
The South
The sun, if we're lucky,
And the moon

The canyon
Deep and wide
Calls to the cosmos

Can you hear me?

This question
Maybe lost in the folds of every echo –
Maybe not -
Makes its way
Across the crayon blue
Into the black
Where the dust and light
Of days gone by
Are cooler now
And falling from the sky

Black Woman
White Woman
Brown Woman

You

Say it

Try again to tell your story
To wring the song out of your skin

Bow when you are finished
Left your soft body fold
At the place where the words
Have been weight
Borrowed stones
Someone asked you to carry

This is the situation,
You see

When the kettle screams
And the dog is done

The door will ask you to walk through it

Courage smells a lot like sweat

(You do not have to leave)

But what about the blacktop birds
And winter skies
And that faces you might find for your stories?

What about the sentences?
The words lined up around the block
Waiting impatiently to be put on your page?

Grab your gun
or your wand
and put on your helmet
Pick up your pen and go

They are waiting
At the gate
To take you
Through the tunnel and the trees

To the light
So bright
With wings and words
To sooth you
Wounded, yes, and also bruised
But healing now
No longer bleeding
They want to show you how

They are waiting
At the gate to help you

She is waving

Stand up and leave your room

Promises kept and flaws forgiven
I guess we start again from here
When was the last time you stayed up late enough to
ache?
I stretch toward something I know I cannot reach
The world bows down to greet me
Agrees to meet me where I am
Down in the dirt in search of something small that I've
forgotten
Or have lost

The night sky kills the day
The dark distracts me from my digging

Empty handed I come home
Empty handed back to the place
Where you are waiting
With the lantern
With the light

This is how the heart behaves:
A parade
A picnic
Sitting four rows from the door
In a church I don't belong to
Up on the roof watching the wildfires with a friend
At a funeral
On the street
Keeping step with perfect strangers
Walking hard against the wind
I have waited for so long
That the grass has grown over
The spot where I stand
And tied me to a place
That I picked
When I was just a kid
Who still hoped that whiskey had the answers
And wrote long lists of things
She thought that she wanted
In a book she hid under the bed

It's been six years
And that doesn't make sense
To anyone
Except for the sun

I keep searching the sky
For signs of life
And so far silence
Is the only thing screaming

No grand gestures I guess
That's not your style
Nothing too hard to believe

Just the sound of the space between your old favorite
songs
As they play one right after the other

Someone was always saying "sit still"
But they didn't see the light on the floor
As it followed their feet
Or the fire that burned everything breathing

A heavy hand on my shoulder
To keep me from moving
A shameful stool in the back of the room

They all did their best
But it wasn't enough
I still spilled into color and sound

A single beam
Of bright light
On black skin
Before a bullet
Tore a hole
Through the heart
Of the world
While we were watching

Speak of a joy
Using all four of your voices
Even the one that sounds like the rain

Look at the beasts and the trees
Free will is a mystery
To the old man in the alley
Who just kissed a stray cat
On the mouth
On the dark edge of dawn
When he thought no one was watching

Yes!

This must mean something special
To the one who imagines this man
And hopes that he's well
Despite what he did
When he was younger

What remains
Stays behind
Still exists
After breath
After bones
Are returned
To the place where they came from

If it's true
What they say
About our bodies being stars

You are proof

Bible bones
Holy
Holy
When Adam lost his rib
A woman rose
And grabbed an apple
And a snake slipped from its skin
Naked as nothing
With nowhere to go
The humans stood inside the shade
Hungry
Hungry
Adam shook his head
And watched the woman while she ate

Up and down
Among the living creatures
Small enough to go unseen
She waits

Quiet as it's kept,
Someone said to me recently,
White people don't really need God

I listened for the bells that day
And looked everyone I met in the eye
Maybe he was wrong

Every face
Framed a story I still do not know
Every head
Seemed to turn toward the light

Follow the fox tracks
You never know what you might find:
Bloated blackberries hanging heavy on an overgrown
bush
An empty space in the coop where the eggs used to be
Golden mushrooms
A rotten apple or plum

Your bare feet kissed the concrete ceremoniously
Your eyes and ears
Your skin
Your teeth
The whole cathedral of your being

All the girls believe in black magic
All the boys believe in blood

Eat my heart
Swallow it whole
Wash me down with whiskey

The lambs dislike
The birds of prey
But this is no surprise

I want to stay soft
So I pray on my knees
In the dark
To a place that I want to believe in

I say your name six times

The birds in the graveyard
Don't know who is dead
The birds in the graveyard
don't care

Your body isn't buried here
You're eighteen -hundred miles away
Still, I come down on some days
to show you new things
and let you know
that we have not forgotten

A woman has a good dream about the future

She finds herself,
Sleeping,
Surrounded by hands
That pull her up through the dirt
Into daylight

She is weightless
In a blue winter coat
That she wore as a child
And muddy boots
That she must have borrowed

When my time came
Someone else's sister showed me what to do:

"You can't wear that brick to ballet."

My blood soaked seat
Gave me away
Another secret I wasn't ready to tell

"Put your foot up on the toilet,"
She whispered through the door.
"It will be easier that way."

Someone else's sister dressed me up
Like a doll for my first dance

"You can wear big earrings or a hair bow, but not
both."

I wore her white gown like a cape
and laced up her hand me down shoes
I let her memories move me on to the dance floor

This story is no longer available.

This is a tale of wild things
Bought
Sold
And traded
In a dark room
In the corner
Where I am still crouched down and careful
Not to disturb the dust
Or make a noise
I am waiting for word
From someone else
That is safe to stand up
And say something true
To raise my arms
Toward the black blue of heaven
I am waving like crazy
My fingers are flashlights
I am shouting your name at the sky

The bougainvillea blooms are beautiful
Even if you were not born here
And came sneaking into town on the back
Of a dream
That started in someone else's basement when you
were ten

Have you ever been on the freeway at dawn and had
the whole place to yourself?

Have you ever seen the city from above,
Sprawled out around you like the limbs of someone
who has fallen backwards into the snow and frozen?

If you still believe that it's a poet's job
To ease your mind in times of war
Then here you go:

The early morning heat can make you crazy
But the cool that comes at midnight might be the cure

I am sitting in the kitchen
While the frozen cookies bake
Thinking about what women need
And say and hope for

I am wondering about the way we work
And want
And learn to live without
All of the things
That we have forgotten how to ask for
And all the trades we make on faith

I've been looking for myself on every corner
And underneath every overturned stone

Remember when we drove
To the farm
With your mom
And I sneezed all night long
And kept everyone up
While the chickens slept up in the trees?
I was homesick

No one ever came to save us
Like we always hoped that they would

In fact,
We lost four more

Your voice
Across decades sounds like home

Your laugh
From faraway
Feels like love

I need you wild
And awake
And willing to dissolve
And disappear into nothing
When the time comes and you are called

I need you healed
And whole hearted
Sun-dried and smelling like every place
That I have been
And want to go
When this war is finally over
And the world returns
To the way that it was
When someone quieter was king

I need you here
And out there
And beside me in the dark
When the dead will be raised
From the dirt of a pine covered valley
Ninety million miles from the sun

I need you ready to run
When they come home to claim
What was theirs
But was taken
All of the women
Who have been lost
And have been touched
And almost loved along the way

I need you wild

The lines around my eyes disappear
When I'm scared
And fool me into thinking
I still can't do it
But I have been here longer
Than I have not been here
Holding steady
Holding tight
Waiting for whatever it was
That I was promised
On a late night long ago
In the middle of the city during summer
I am here

There is love there
They told me
Before they dropped me into the arms of a world I'd
never heard of

You will enjoy the grey light of early morning
And city snails and tall grass and the way the wind will
feel on your skin
When it's warm out

You will meet people there
And animals
And find that both will want to take to your bed

You will hear the sound of six thousand guitars
And stand on bridges and boats
And build homes in new towns with kind strangers
You will live in the desert and walk to the water
And sleep on the side of a mountain

There are books there, they said,
And their pages will save you
From time and pain and terror and news of wars that
you will not understand
And old laws you did not write but must follow
Or else
Until it's over

The devil himself made me do it
The old fashioned black magic of love
My heart is wandering worried
Out of its mind
Looking for a pump to plug into

I am not a goddess
Running naked through the trees
Who will have me?

Unwild and unwilling to repent
I am watching very closely
Wearing black top tennis shoes
Thick with tar and time

I am listening
And listening

Taking notes on what it means to be alive

I remember reading once
in a poem
or a prayer
"We are the birds that stay"
but when I searched tonight for the line
I could not find it

(We are the birds that stay)

That was a very long list of goodbyes
and letting go
and looking again for faraway faces that you used to
see everyday
before they disappeared into the distance of death
and big things and adventure and babies
and cross town traffic and time
but this place:

Here

With the birds that have stayed
This place
Now
In the morning

Stare at the world
And the world stares back

God, she said,
is the way that the Atlantic Ocean
Spit me out when I was drowning
When I was just a little girl

I dreamt again that I was in a room
without books
But wasn't scared
I knew enough about life by then to survive it

Have you ever noticed how the rain that was slamming
outside your windows while you were sleeping always
seems to slow down before dawn?

Right here
In the land of high hopes
We go broke
And crack bones
And bake cakes made with summer fresh berries
We belong to each other
And bring little gifts
To the widow that waits
For a car that will never come home
We laugh out loud during wartime
And try not to take to the mean city streets screaming
We go on
And on
And keep going
We stretch and bend
And fall back into grass
We stare bravely
Up into the blue

When Light,
God's eldest daughter,
Walks into the room
The bone cold feet of darkness
Disappear
And every day
This ordinary turn
Surprises you
Every day
You weep alone
On thankful knees
That still believed she wouldn't show
But here she is

This is the sound of my own body breathing
Deep
Like the footprints
Of one who has jumped from above
And survived it
There is still so much to see here

This part is ours
And we own it
No one can take it away

We used to wonder what would happen
If we packed up and moved
We used to worry

We stand now
In new places
Wearing the truth
Of time passed
And holding on
To every hand that will have us

We don't wait anymore
We won't waste it

We wake up in the morning
Alive

In the low light
In the morning
At the soft blue edge of day

Some,
Still dreaming,
Will miss it
The moment when
what has already happened
slips out of our hands
and whatever will be next is born

Remember how we used to sleep so late
when we were kids?
How sometimes we would stay inside until noon?

Please
give us the right language
for whatever this is

Please
give us the gift
of good healing

The light illuminates particulates -
the fertile pollen of a life
lived in the privilege of captivity
Old skin safely shed
every second
waking up to the song birds
brand new

She is writing something beautiful
about touch and skin and hips
She is reading the book of her bare feet again
because the only bones she wants to study
are her own
When she makes a full moon with her mouth
I am watching through her window
When she looks to me
I wave
I listen closely for her poetry
from here

These hands
washed raw
still bleed and make things
These hands
still know what to say
Fine fingers
(ten)
covered in paint
turn to the pen for a kiss or a handshake
and bring the whole world
right back into being

Let the backyard birds be your mother now
Let them teach you how to be

ANNE CARMACK

Acknowledgments

MY OWN BODY BREATHING would not have turned into the book that you hold in your hands without the help of my dear friend and mentor, the writer and teacher, Pixie Lighthorse. It was Pixie who suggested that it was finally time to put this poetry collection together and my deep trust in her voice and her vision let me believe her. Her willingness to share her creative resources, network connections and knowledge put me right where I needed to be. I owe a debt of gratitude to her and her creative team and hope to some day return this fine favor.

Anne Carmack is a bi-racial, Midwestern born, Los Angeles based, self-taught writer, and multidisciplinary artist. Determined to celebrate the ordinary beauty of everyday things as evidenced by her poetic and photographic fascination with back alley trash and found treasures, her search for something still undefined continues.

www.annecarmackstudio.com

Made in the USA
San Bernardino, CA
25 June 2020

74146246R00035